Entertain in style—with THE GOURMET BLENDER COOKBOOK! The secret is in your blender and over a hundred pages of recipes for soups, salads, entrees, sauces, drinks, and desserts.

Make complicated sauces or frothy drinks in seconds. Whip up a fondue, a mousse, or a vichyssoisse in minutes. Amaze and mystify your friends and family with your overnight mastery of haute cuisine.

The new, instant, switched-on cookery is here!

THE
GOURMET
BLENDER
COOKBOOK

by William I. Kaufman

Illustrations by Richard Smith

Galahad Books   New York City

Library of Congress Catalog Card Number: 76-15148
ISBN: 0-88365-156-4

Published by arrangement with Pyramid Communications, Inc.
919 Third Avenue, New York, N.Y. 10022

Manufactured in the United States of America

These recipes first appeared in THE NEW BLENDER COOKBOOK
by William I. Kaufman, published by Pyramid Publications,
January 1969

CONTENTS

Turn the page for more blender treats

CONTENTS (continued)

Just the right touch to enhance any entree—curry, cranberry, or sharp tartare.

Green salads perk up immediately with these zesty blue cheese, French, or avocado accompaniments.

The staff of life in every form, from rich hearty loaves to light-as-air pancakes.

The way to a man's heart is through feather-light cakes, extra-rich pies, and buttery cookies.

Perfect-every-time soufflés, mousses, parfaits, ice cream—and more!

A luscious complement—caramel, butterscotch, chocolate — to the well turned out dessert.

A full range of refreshing beverages, from traditional daiquiris and bacardis to the "Queen of the Islands" and the "Czarina's Delight."

PREFACE

The electric blender has brought about a happy miracle in the kitchen. Now the busiest housewife or career woman can treat her family or please her guests with gourmet dishes whipped up in practically no time at all. The flick of a switch does the scullery work and the "cook" takes the credit.

Imagine setting out a Deluxe Shrimp Pâté, Chilled Minted Pea Soup, Lobster Mousse, and topping it all off with Chocolate Rum Parfaits, after your guests have already been delighted by tall drinks from your blender. The preparation of these classic dishes is child's play with the help of your blender and the easy-to-follow recipes collected here.

Every aspect of epicurean cookery—from exotic appetizers to super-rich desserts—is covered in this GOURMET BLENDER COOKBOOK. To add excitement to the lowly vegetable dish and eye-appeal to the molded salad, to make soups and sauces smooth and creamy, and to render cooling drinks even more refreshing, you will want to keep this handy book close to your blender.

It's easy to be a master chef and it's fun! With these foolproof recipes and the touch of a button the magic is right at your fingertips.

WILLIAM I. KAUFMAN

SPREADS & DIPS

LIVER PATE

2 tablespoons butter	1 hard-cooked egg, quartered
½ pound chicken livers	1 teaspoon lemon juice
1 medium onion, sliced	½ teaspoon salt
1 clove garlic, split	¼ teaspoon pepper
¼ cup mayonnaise	

Melt butter over medium heat. **Add** chicken livers. **Saute** about 5 minutes until tender. **Add** onion and garlic. **Cook** 2 minutes over low heat until onion is soft. **Place** all ingredients in blender container. **Cover and process** until smooth. **Stop Blender** and scrape down sides of container, if necessary. **Refrigerate** until serving. **Makes:** 1½ cups.

LOBSTER SPREAD

1 cup cooked lobster meat, cubed	3 hard-cooked eggs
¼ cup mayonnaise	

Place all ingredients in blender container. **Cover and Process** until smooth. **Stop Blender** and scrape down sides of container with rubber spatula, if necessary. **Makes:** about 1½ cups.

11

YULE CHEESE BALL

½ cup pecans
6 sprigs parsley
¼ cup milk
1 package (3 ounces) blue cheese, cubed
¼ cup Cheddar cheese, cubed

1 small wedge onion
1 teaspoon Worcestershire sauce
2 packages (3 ounces each) cream cheese, cubed
Crackers

Place pecans and parsley in blender container. **Cover and Process** until coarsely chopped. **Remove** from container. **Place**, milk and blue cheese in blender container. **Cover and Process** on high speed about 5 seconds. With blender continuing to run, **Remove** feeder cap and slowly add Cheddar cheese. Add onion, Worcestershire sauce and cream cheese. **Cover and Process** on high speed until smooth. **Stop Blender** and scrape down sides of container with rubber spatula, if necessary. **Remove** from container and shape into a ball. **Refrigerate** overnight. Roll cheese ball in pecan-parsley mixture before serving on crackers. **Makes:** one 3″ ball.

BAVARIAN CHIP DIP

1 package (3 ounces) cream cheese,
   softened at room temperature
2 tablespoons lemon juice
1 package (8 ounces) Braunschweiger
   (liver sausage)

1 envelope dried onion soup mix
1 tablespoon prepared horseradish
1 teaspoon Worcestershire sauce
Dash of Tabasco
⅔ cup evaporated milk

Combine cream cheese and lemon juice in blender container. **Cover and Process** until smooth. **Add** remaining ingredients. **Cover and Process** at high speed until completely blended. **Chill** before serving. **Makes:** approximately 2 cups.

AVOCADO DIP

1 ripe avocado, peeled and cubed
1 tablespoon lemon juice
1 thin slice onion
⅛ teaspoon salt

Dash Worcestershire sauce
3 ounces cream cheese, softened and
cut in small pieces

Place all ingredients except cream cheese in blender container. **Cover and Process** on high speed to purée until smooth. With blender continuing to run, **Remove** feeder cap and slowly add cream cheese. **Cover and Process** until smooth. **Chill** before serving. **Makes:** 1 cup.

SHRIMP-CUCUMBER SPREAD

2 tablespoons chili sauce
1 thin wedge lemon, peeled and seeded
Dash Worcestershire sauce
¼ teaspoon dill seed

1 package (3 ounces) soft cream cheese, cubed
¼ peeled cucumber, cut up
1 cup (approximately 1 small can) cleaned, cooked shrimp

Place chili sauce, lemon, Worcestershire sauce, dill seed and cream cheese in blender container. **Cover and Process** until smooth. **Add** cucumber and shrimp and continue to process until chopped. **Stop Blender** and scrape down sides of container with rubber spatula, if necessary. **Serve** on caraway rye bread or whole-wheat bread. **Makes:** 6 to 8 sandwiches.

HERB BUTTER

½ cup soft butter
1 teaspoon lemon juice

¾ teaspoon thyme, rosemary, basil or tarragon

Place all ingredients in blender container. **Cover and Process** at low speed until smooth. **Stop Blender** and scrape down sides of container with rubber spatula, if necessary. **Makes:** ½ cup.

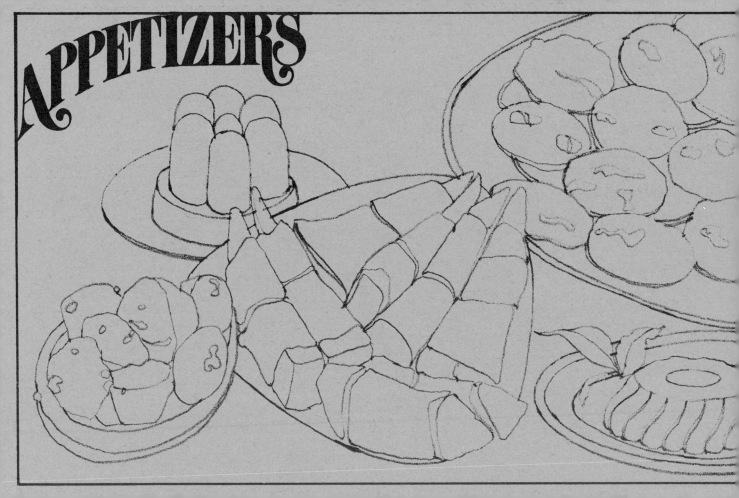

APPETIZERS

MOLDED PATE

3 tablespoons brandy
1 can (3 or 4 ounces) chopped
   mushrooms
½ pound chicken livers
1 can condensed beef bouillon, divided

1 envelope unflavored gelatine
1 teaspoon Worcestershire sauce
½ cup pitted ripe olives
¼ cup parsley leaves
¼ teaspoon nutmeg
Wafers or toast

Combine brandy and liquid from mushrooms in small saucepan. **Add** chicken livers. **Bring** to a boil. **Cook** rapidly until livers are done and liquid has evaporated, about 5 minutes. **Pour** ¼ cup bouillon in blender container. **Sprinkle** gelatine over liquid. Allow to soften. **Heat** ½ cup bouillon to a boil. **Add** to blender. **Cover and Process** at proper speed for gelatine (low) until gelatine dissolves. If gelatine granules cling to container, use a rubber spatula to push them into the mixture. **Add** remaining bouillon, mushrooms, chicken livers and other ingredients. **Cover and Process** at high speed until smooth. **Pour** into 3-cup mold or 2 small molds. **Chill** until firm, several hours or overnight. **Unmold** and serve with crisp wafers or toast. **Makes:** 2½ cups.

TARAMA

⅔ cup red caviar
¼ small onion
4 sprigs parsley
Juice of 1 lemon

2 slices fresh bread, broken in 1-inch pieces
1 cup olive oil
Toast fingers or crackers

Place caviar in blender container with onion, parsley and lemon juice. **Cover and Process** only until mixture is smooth. **Add** bread, a little at a time. **Then Add** olive oil very gradually, adding only enough to make mixture stiff like mayonnaise. **Keep** in refrigerator for about a week. **Serve** with toast fingers or crackers. **Makes:** 1¾ cups.

APPETIZER ESCOFFIER

½ soup can water
1 small onion, cut in half
12 mint leaves
1 garlic clove

1 cup heavy cream
1 can (11¼ ounces) condensed green pea soup

Combine water, onion, mint leaves and garlic in blender container. **Cover and Process** until smooth. **Add Soup** and reprocess. **Chill** 24 hours. **Stir** in 1 cup heavy cream. **Makes:** 4 servings.

DELUXE SHRIMP PATE

3 to 4 tablespoons Pernod
Juice of ½ lemon
½ teaspoon mace
Dash Tabasco
1 teaspoon prepared mustard

¼ pound butter, softened
Salt and pepper to taste
1 pound shrimp, cooked, shelled
Toast triangles

Place all ingredients except shrimp in blender container. **Cover and Process** to blend. **Remove** feeder cap and add 3 or 4 shrimp at a time until coarsely chopped. **Stop Blender** and scrape down sides of container with rubber spatula, if necessary. **Turn** mixture into mold or bowl and chill. **Serve** with toast triangles. **Makes:** 2 cups.

CURRIED EGG BALLS

1 slice bread, cut in 1-inch pieces	¼ teaspoon curry powder
¼ cup nuts	¼ teaspoon salt
¼ cup mayonnaise	Dash of pepper
6 hard-cooked eggs, quartered	2 tablespoons butter

Place bread and nuts in blender container. **Cover and Process** as for nuts until finely grated. Set aside. **Place** remaining ingredients, except butter, in blender container. **Cover and Process** until smooth. **Shape** into ½-inch balls. **Brown** crumb mixture in butter. **Roll** egg balls in crumb mixture. **Store** in refrigerator. **Makes:** about 2 dozen balls.

SOUPS

LA BONNE SOUPE AU POULET

1½ cups cooked chicken or turkey,
   divided
2 cups chicken broth
1 small onion, chopped fine
3 tablespoons butter

2 tablespoons parsley
1 teaspoon fresh tarragon leaves or
   ⅓ teaspoon dried tarragon
1 cup heavy cream (cold)
Finely cut parsley for garnish

Place 1 cup fine-cut white meat and broth in blender container. **Cover and Process** to blend thoroughly. **Saute** onion in butter, then add to blender container with rest of chicken, parsley, and tarragon. **Cover and Process** to blend thoroughly. **Chill. Add** cream. **Chill** again just before serving. **Garnish** with finely cut parsley and chives. **Makes:** 4 servings.

GAZPACHO

Ingredients
2 cans (10½ ounces each)
  condensed tomato soup
1 to 2 cloves garlic
1 medium onion, sliced
1 small green pepper, seeded
  and cut in pieces
1 soup can water
2 cups tomato juice
Dash black pepper
Tabasco

Garnishes
1 cucumber, seeded (cut in half
  lengthwise and scrape out seeds
  with spoon)
1 green pepper, seeded
1 onion
3 celery stalks
1 ripe tomato
Croutons cooked in garlic butter

Place one can of soup in blender container with garlic, onion and pepper, **Cover and Process** to purée. **Combine** in bowl with remaining soup, water and tomato juice. **Season** to taste with pepper and Tabasco. **Chill** thoroughly. **Serve** each guest a bowl of soup garnished with vegetables which have been chopped fine and chilled. **Makes:** 6 servings.

WHITE MOUNTAIN REFRESHER

1 can (10½ ounces) frozen
   condensed cream of potato soup
1 soup can water

½ cup sour cream
¼ cup finely chopped cucumber

Combine soup and water in saucepan. **Cook** over low heat until soup is thawed. **Stir** now and then. **Place** in blender container. **Cover and Process** until smooth. **Stir** in sour cream and cucumber and reprocess. **Chill** in refrigerator at least 4 hours. **Serve** in chilled bowls. **Makes:** 3 servings.

VICHYSSOISE

1 can (10½ ounces) frozen
   condensed cream of potato soup
½ soup can milk

½ soup can light cream
Garnishes

Place soup, milk and cream in saucepan and cook over low heat until soup is completely thawed. **Stir** now and then. **Place** in blender container. **Cover and Process** until smooth. **Chill** in refrigerator for at least 4 hours before serving. **Serve** in chilled bowls. **Garnish** with any of the following: minced chives, minced green pepper, minced parsley, shredded process or grated Parmesan cheese, shredded beets, sliced stuffed olives, minced celery, thinly sliced radishes, chopped cucumber or shredded carrot. **Makes:** 3 servings.

ENCORE SOUP

1 can (1 pound) cut green beans
¼ cup butter or margarine
1 cup sliced fresh mushrooms
1 tablespoon flour
½ teaspoon salt

¼ teaspoon tarragon
⅛ teaspoon basil
⅛ teaspoon white pepper
Few dashes dry mustard
1 cup milk

Place beans in liquid in blender container. **Cover and Process** as for vegetables until smooth. **Melt** butter in large saucepan. **Add** mushrooms and sauté until tender. **Remove** from pan with slotted spoon. **Blend** flour, salt, tarragon, basil, white pepper and mustard into butter in saucepan. **Mix** in bean purée and milk. **Cook** over low heat, stirring constantly, until mixture comes to boil and is slightly thickened. **Add** mushrooms. **Serve. Makes:** 4 to 6 servings.

BROCCOLI CHEESE SOUP

1 package (10 ounces)
frozen broccoli
½ cup boiling water
1 teaspoon salt
4 tablespoons butter or margarine
¼ cup finely minced onion

3 tablespoons flour
1 quart milk
1 cup shredded American cheese
⅛ teaspoon pepper
Additional shredded cheese for garnish

Cook broccoli according to package directions in water and salt. **Place** broccoli and liquid in blender container. **Cover and Process** to purée. **Set Aside. Meanwhile, melt** butter in saucepan. **Add** onion and sauté until tender. **Blend** in flour. **Add** milk, stirring constantly. **Cook and Stir** until sauce is smooth and thickened. **Add** cheese, pepper and broccoli purée. **Stir** until cheese is melted. **Serve** hot. **Garnish** with shreds of cheese. **Makes:** 6 servings.

CHILLED MINTED PEA SOUP

1 can (11¼ ounces) condensed
   green pea soup
1 soup can milk

¼ cup light cream
½ teaspoon dried mint flakes,
   crushed

Place all ingredients in blender container. **Cover and Process** until smooth. **Chill** at least 4 hours before serving. **Makes:** 3 to 4 servings.

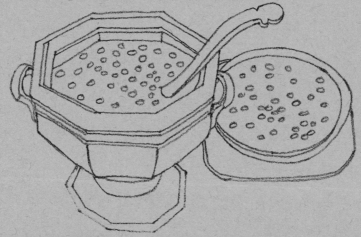

SALADS

DELTA SUNSET MOLD

2 envelopes unflavored gelatine
¼ teaspoon salt
1½ cups (12 ounces) regular or low-calorie orange soda, divided
2 fresh Bartlett pears, pared, cored and cubed

1 tablespoon lemon juice
1 cup plain yoghurt
1 tablespoon grated orange rind
Salad greens
Additional pear slices for garnish

Combine gelatine, salt and ½ cup soda in top of a double boiler. **Place** over hot water and stir until dissolved. **Cool** slightly. **Coat** pear cubes with lemon juice. **Place** pears in blender container with 1 cup soda and yoghurt. **Cover and Process** until smooth. **Fold** in gelatine mixture and orange rind. **Turn** into 4-cup mold. **Chill** until firm. **Unmold** onto serving plate. **Garnish** with greens and additional pear slices, if desired. **Makes:** 5 servings.

CARROT CAROUSEL

2 envelopes unflavored gelatine
1½ cups cold orange juice divided
½ cup boiling orange juice
¼ teaspoon salt
1 cup salad dressing

1½ cups carrot pieces
1⅔ cups (13½-ounce can)
    crushed pineapple, undrained
Watercress and carrot curls for garnish

Sprinkle gelatine over ½ cup cold orange juice in blender container. Allow to stand while assembling remaining ingredients. **Add** boiling orange juice. **Cover and Process** at proper speed for gelatine (low) until gelatine dissolves. If gelatine granules cling to the sides of the container, use a rubber spatula to push them into the mixture. When gelatine is dissolved, **Add** remaining 1 cup cold orange juice, salt and salad dressing. **Process** until well blended. **Stop Blender and Add** carrot pieces. **Cover and Process** as for raw vegetables until carrots are finely grated. **Stir** in pineapple and syrup. **Turn** into 6-cup mold. **Chill** until firm. **Unmold. Garnish** with watercress and carrot curls. **Makes:** 8 servings.

PATIO COLESLAW

2 envelopes unflavored gelatine
½ cup cold water
1 cup boiling water
1 teaspoon salt
2 tablespoons lemon juice
1 cup salad dressing
1 medium onion, quartered

2 cups cabbage pieces
1 cup celery pieces
1 cup cucumber pieces (peeled)
1 can (4 ounces) pimiento,
   drained and diced
Cherry tomatoes for garnish

Sprinkle gelatine over cold water in blender container. Allow to stand while assembling remaining ingredients. **Add** boiling water. **Cover and Process** at proper speed for gelatine (low) until gelatine dissolves. If gelatine granules cling to the sides of the container, use a rubber spatula to push them into the mixture. When gelatine is dissolved, **Add** salt, lemon juice and salad dressing. **Continue to Process** until well blended. **Stop Blender** and add onion. **Cover and Process** until finely chopped. **Stop Blender and Add** cabbage, celery and cucumber pieces. **Cover and Process** only until all pieces are coarsely chopped. **Chill** until mixture is slightly thickened. **Stir** in diced pimiento. **Turn** into 6-cup mold. **Chill** until firm. **Unmold**. **Garnish** with cherry tomatoes. **Makes:** 8 servings.

CREAMY CUCUMBER MOLD

1 package (3 ounces) lime-flavored
  gelatin
½ cup hot water
1 cup mayonnaise
1 cup sour cream

1 tablespoon lemon juice
¼ teaspoon salt
1 medium unpared cucumber,
  cut in 2-inch pieces
½ medium onion, quartered

Place gelatine and hot water in blender container. **Cover and Process** at proper speed for gelatine (low) until gelatine dissolves. **Add** mayonnaise, sour cream, lemon juice and salt. **Cover and Process** until smooth. With blender continuing to run, **Remove** feeder cap from lid, and slowly add cucumber and onion. **Cover and Process** until finely chopped. **Turn** into 3-cup mold. **Chill** until firm. **Makes:** 4 to 6 servings.

FROZEN PEACH AND PECAN SALAD

1 cup heavy cream
1 cup mayonnaise
2 packages (3 ounces each)
   cream cheese, cubed

1 cup pecans
8 peach halves

Blender-Whip cream. **Empty** into large bowl and reserve. **Place** mayonnaise in blender container. **Cover and Process** to blend. **Remove** feeder cap and gradually add cheese. **Cover and Continue Processing** until smooth. **Add** pecans. **Cover and Process** to chop (only a few seconds). **Fold** the blended mixture into the whipped cream. **Arrange** peach halves, hollow side up, in refrigerator tray. **Pour** cheese and cream mixture over peach halves. **Cover** tightly with aluminum foil and freeze until firm. **Thaw** before serving. **Makes:** 8 servings.

SPINACH IN ORANGE BUTTER SAUCE

2 packages (10 ounces each)
  frozen chopped spinach
1 egg yolk
½ tablespoon lemon juice

Few grains cayenne
¼ cup melted butter, bubbling hot
¼ teaspoon grated orange rind
2 tablespoons orange juice

Cook spinach according to package directions. **Meanwhile Place** egg yolk, lemon juice, and cayenne in blender container. **Cover and Process** on low. **Remove Cover and Add** slowly, in a thin stream, ¼ cup melted butter. When all butter has been added, **Stop Blender. Stir** in grated orange rind and juice. **Drain** cooked spinach thoroughly. **Add** orange butter sauce. **Makes:** 6 servings.

SEA BREEZE SPINACH MOLD

2 envelopes unflavored gelatine
¼ cup cold water
1 can (10½ ounces) condensed beef broth, divided
¼ teaspoon salt
2 tablespoons lemon juice
1 cup salad dressing
1 medium onion, quartered

1 package (10 ounces) frozen chopped spinach, thawed
4 hard-cooked eggs, quartered
½ pound bacon, crisply cooked and crumbled
Pimiento strips for garnish

Sprinkle gelatine over cold water and ¼ cup beef broth in blender container. Allow to stand while assembling remaining ingredients. **Heat** remaining beef broth to boiling. **Add** to blender container and process at proper speed for gelatine (low) until gelatine dissolves. If any gelatine granules cling to the sides of the container, use a rubber spatula to push them into the mixture. When gelatine is dissolved, **Add** salt, lemon juice and salad dressing. **Continue to Process** until well blended. **Stop Blender** and add onion. **Cover and Process** until onion is chopped. **Stop Blender** and add spinach and eggs. **Cover and Process** just until eggs are coarsely chopped. **Stir** in bacon. **Turn** into 6-cup mold. **Chill** until firm. **Unmold. Garnish** with pimiento strips. **Makes:** 8 servings.

POTATO KUGEL

4 cups cubed potatoes
3 eggs
1 large onion, quartered
1½ teaspoons salt

¼ teaspoon pepper
¼ cup melted chicken fat
⅓ cup potato flour
6 sprigs parsley (stems removed)

Preheat oven to 350°F. **Place** potatoes in blender container. **Add** cold water to cover. **Cover and Process** on high speed only a few seconds, until potatoes are grated. **Remove** potatoes from blender container. **Drain** well. **Place** remaining ingredients in blender container in the order listed. **Cover and Process** until parsley is chopped. **Mix** batter thoroughly with well-drained potatoes. **Turn** into greased 1½ quart casserole. **Bake** 1 hour or until brown. **Serve** hot. **Makes:** 6 to 8 servings.

BROCCOLI MOLD

2 envelopes unflavored gelatine
½ cup cold water
1 cup boiling water
4 chicken bouillon cubes
1 cup salad dressing
1 tablespoon lemon juice

½ medium onion, quartered
1 package (10 ounces) frozen chopped broccoli, cooked 2 to 3 minutes and drained
¼ cup grated Parmesan cheese
Sliced tomatoes

Sprinkle gelatine over cold water in blender container. Allow to stand while assembling remaining ingredients. **Add** boiling water and bouillon cubes. **Cover and Process** at proper speed for gelatine (low) until gelatine dissolves. If gelatine granules cling to the sides of the container, use a rubber spatula to push them into the mixture. When gelatine is dissolved, **Add** salad dressing and lemon juice. **Cover and Process** until smooth. **Add** onion, broccoli and cheese. **Process** just until onion and broccoli are coarsely chopped. **Turn** into 4-cup mold. **Chill** until firm. **Unmold** and serve with sliced tomatoes. **Makes:** 8 servings.

CUCUMBER MOUSSE

1 large or 2 small cucumbers,
 peeled and cut in 1-inch pieces
1 envelope unflavored gelatine
¼ cup cold water
2 tablespoons boiling water
1 tablespoon lemon juice

6 tablespoons mayonnaise
1 teaspoon Worcestershire sauce
1 teaspoon salt
Dash of white pepper
1 cup creamed cottage cheese
Green food coloring, optional

Place cucumber in blender container. **Cover and Process** to purée until smooth. Use only 1½ cups of puréed cucumber. **Soften** gelatine in cold water in blender container and add hot water. **Cover and Process** at proper speed for gelatine (low) until gelatine dissolves. **Add** cucumber and remaining ingredients. **Cover and Process** on high speed until smooth. (If desired tint the mixture a pale green with a few drops of food coloring.) **Pour** into 1-quart mold or into 8 individual molds. **Chill** until firm. **Unmold** onto serving plate or individual plates. **Makes:** 8 servings.

CURRIED RICE RING

1 cup melted butter
1 medium onion, cut up
½ green pepper, cut up
1 can (4 ounces) pimiento
1 can (13 ounces) tomato consomme

¾ cup water
¼ teaspoon monosodium glutamate
⅛ teaspoon pepper
1 cup raw quick cooking rice

Place butter, cut-up onion, green pepper, pimiento, consommé, water and seasoning in blender container. **Cover and Process** until vegetables are coarsely chopped. **Pour** into heavy skillet. **Stir** in rice. **Cover** tightly. **Cook** over medium heat 8 to 10 minutes until rice is cooked. Pack firmly into buttered ring mold, then unmold. **Pour** Egg-Mushroom* Filling into center of mold. **Makes:** 6 to 8 servings.

*Egg-Mushroom Filling

½ pound fresh mushrooms
2 tablespoons butter
2 tablespoons flour
¼ teaspoon salt
1 cup milk

¼ cup sharp Cheddar cheese, cubed
1 tablespoon chili sauce
½ teaspoon curry powder
5 hard cooked eggs, cut in eighths

Clean mushrooms. **Saute** in butter in skillet until soft. **Remove** mushrooms to a large mixing bowl. **Add** more butter, if needed, to skillet to make 2 tablespoons. **Add** flour and salt and stir. **Add** milk and cook over low heat, stirring constantly, for about 3 minutes. **Pour** sauce into blender container. **Add** cheese, chili sauce and curry powder. **Cover and Process** until smooth. **Add** cut-up eggs to mushrooms in mixing bowl. **Pour** blended mixture over eggs and mushrooms. **Stir** until well-mixed. **Pour** into center of rice ring.

BAKED RICE FLUFF

2 cups rice
3 eggs, separated
¼ medium onion, cut up

½ cup butter, melted
1 cup sharp Cheddar cheese, cubed
1 cup parsley

Preheat oven to 350°F. **Cook** rice according to package directions and set aside in mixing bowl. **Place** egg yolks in blender container with onion and butter. **Cover and Begin Processing.** While blending, **Add** cheese. **Process** until smooth. **Add** parsley and process only long enough to chop. If mixture clings to sides of container, use rubber spatula to push mixture down into blades. **Pour** over cooked rice and mix thoroughly. **Beat** egg whites with rotary beater until stiff. **Fold** into rice mixture. **Bake** 25 minutes. **Serve** alone or with creamed seafood. **Makes:** 4 servings.

SAUCY PINK CAULIFLOWER

2 packages (10 ounces each)
   frozen cauliflower
1 jar (4 ounces) pimiento, drained
1 cup milk

2 tablespoons butter or margarine
2 tablespoons flour
½ teaspoon salt

Cook cauliflower according to package directions. **Drain** and keep warm. **Place** pimiento and milk in blender container. **Process** until smooth. **Melt** butter or margarine in 1 quart saucepan over low heat. **Stir** in flour and salt. **Add** pimiento mixture. **Cook** and stir constantly until thick and bubbly. **Pour** sauce over cauliflower so some of white flowerettes show. **Makes:** 6 servings.

MAIN DISHES

LOBSTER OR CRABMEAT MOUSSE

1 envelope unflavored gelatine
¼ cup cold water
1 pound cooked or canned lobster
    pieces or crabmeat
1 can (10½ ounces) condensed
    cream of mushroom soup
⅓ cup whipping cream

½ cup consommé
2 to 4 drops Tabasco
2 teaspoons lemon juice
Dash nutmeg
Hard-cooked egg slices, truffles,
    red pimiento for garnish

Soften gelatine in cold water. **Place** ⅓ of lobster, mushroom soup and cream in blender container. **Cover and Process** until a fine paste. **Empty** into bowl. **Repeat** process until all lobster, mushroom soup and cream is used. **Combine** consommé with softened gelatine. **Cook,** stirring constantly, over low heat, until gelatine dissolves. **Add** to lobster mixture with seasonings. **Turn** into 1-quart mold which has been moistened with consommé. **Refrigerate** 4 to 6 hours. **Unmold** and decorate with hard-cooked egg slices, truffles and red pimientos. **Makes:** 4 servings.

SHRIMP MOUSSE ELEGANTE

2 egg whites
2 cups heavy cream
Rounded teaspoon salt
½ teaspoon white pepper

¼ teaspoon nutmeg
1 pound shrimp (raw),
   cleaned and deveined

Preheat oven to 350°F. **Combine** egg whites, cream and seasonings in mixing bowl. **Pour** ⅓ of this mixture into blender container. **Add** ⅓ of shrimp. **Cover and Process** to a smooth paste. If any of the mixture clings to sides of container, use a rubber spatula to aid in processing. **Turn** into well-buttered 1-quart mold. **Repeat** process until all ingredients are used. **Cover** mold with aluminum foil. **Place** in pan with 1 inch of water and bake 45 minutes. **Let Stand** in mold 5 minutes. **Turn out** on warm platter and cover with Sauce Elegante.* **Makes** 4 to 6 servings.

*Sauce Elegante

1 can (10½ ounces) condensed
  cream of mushroom soup
⅓ cup dry white Bordeaux wine
1 tablespoon butter
½ teaspoon tarragon (optional)

Dash black pepper
2 sprigs parsley
¼ pound shrimp (cooked),
  cleaned and deveined

Combine all ingredients in blender container. **Cover and Process** only until shrimp are chopped. **Pour** into saucepan. **Heat** slowly until hot. **Pour Over** Shrimp Mousse Elegante. **Makes:** about 2¼ cups.

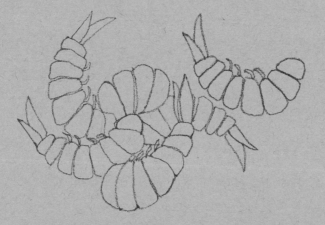

CREAMED OYSTERS

1 pint oysters
3 slices white bread, crusts removed, divided
1 cup hot milk, divided
2 tablespoons butter

$\frac{1}{2}$ teaspoon salt
$\frac{1}{8}$ teaspoon paprika
$\frac{1}{2}$ teaspoon Worcestershire sauce
1 teaspoon sherry
Patty shells or toast

Drain oysters. **Break** one slice bread in blender container. **Add** about ¼ cup hot milk, butter and seasonings. **Cover and Process.** With blender running, **Add** remaining bread broken into small pieces and remaining milk. **Process** until creamy and smooth. **Pour** into saucepan and cook over high heat until mixture comes to boil. **Lower Heat** and add oysters. **Cook** over low heat 10 minutes. (Do not allow sauce to boil.) **Serve** in patty shells or on buttered toast. **Makes:** 3 to 4 servings.

NORWEGIAN FISH PUDDING

1 tablespoon flour
1 teaspoon salt
Dash pepper
⅛ teaspoon nutmeg
1 egg

3 tablespoons softened butter
¼ cup cream
1 pound trout or haddock, fresh or
frozen, cut in pieces
Lemon or tartar sauce

Preheat oven to 325°F. **Place** all ingredients except fish and lemon or tartar sauce in blender container. **Cover and Process** until smooth. **Gradually Add** uncooked fish and process until smooth. If mixture clings to sides of container use rubber spatula to push mixture down into blades. **Turn** into a greased loaf pan and bake ½ hour, or until center is firm. **Serve** with lemon or tartar sauce. **Makes:** 4 servings.

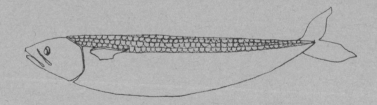

QUICHE LORRAINE

1 9-inch pie crust, unbaked	1½ cups light cream
½ pound bacon, fried crisp, drained and crumbled	½ teaspoon salt
	⅛ teaspoon onion salt
6 ounces Swiss cheese, cubed	Dash nutmeg
3 eggs	Dash pepper

Preheat oven to 375°F. **Sprinkle** bacon over bottom of pie crust. **Place** half cheese in blender container. **Cover and Process** until finely grated. **Sprinkle** over bacon. **Repeat** with rest of cheese. **Place** remaining ingredients in blender container. **Cover and Process** at low speed until just combined, but not foamy. **Pour** mixture into pie shell. **Bake** 35 to 40 minutes or until golden brown and firm. **Remove** from oven. **Let Stand** 5 to 10 minutes before serving. **Makes:** 6 servings.

CHEESE FONDUE

1 pound Swiss cheese, cubed
2 tablespoons flour
1 clove garlic
2 cups dry white wine
⅛ teaspoon ground nutmeg
¼ teaspoon salt

Dash pepper
3 tablespoons Kirsch
Italian or French bread broken into
   bite-sized pieces to be
   dipped in fondue

Place 1 cup Swiss cheese in blender container. **Cover and Process** until coarsely grated. **Empty** into bowl. **Repeat** as above with remaining cheese. **Add** flour to cheese and toss lightly. **Rub** skillet with garlic. **Add** wine to skillet. **Cook** over low heat until wine starts to boil. **Slowly Add** cheese, stirring constantly, until mixture is smooth. Keep temperature low. **Add** nutmeg, salt, pepper and Kirsch. **Heat** through. **Serve** from skillet or chafing dish. **Makes:** 4 cups.

TAHITIAN PORK CHOPS

8 pork chops
¾ cup sherry or other white wine
¼ cup soy sauce
¼ cup salad oil

1 clove garlic
¾ teaspoon ginger
¼ teaspoon oregano
1 tablespoon maple syrup

Preheat oven to 350°F. **Brown** pork chops in skillet. **Place** in baking dish. **Place** all other ingredients in blender container. **Cover and Process** until smooth. **Pour** over chops. **Cover. Bake** 1 to 1½ hours or until tender. **Turn** chops once during baking time to give both sides added browning. **Makes:** 8 servings.

FRENCH HAM AND CHEESE PUFF

1 pound cooked ham, cubed
½ pound Swiss cheese, cubed
½ cup mayonnaise
1 teaspoon prepared mustard
Dash Worcestershire sauce

Dash onion salt
12 slices French bread
6 eggs
2½ cups milk

Preheat oven to 325°F. **Place** half of ham in blender container. **Cover and Process** until finely chopped. **Empty** into bowl. **Repeat** with remaining ham. **Place** half of Swiss cheese in blender container. **Cover and Process** until finely grated. **Empty** into bowl containing ham. **Repeat** with remaining cheese. **Mix** ham and cheese lightly with mayonnaise, mustard, Worcestershire sauce and onion salt. **Spread** mixture on six slices of French bread. **Top** with remaining bread to make six sandwiches. **Place** eggs and milk in blender container. **Cover and Process** until combined. **Pour** mixture over sandwiches. **Cover and Refrigerate** at least 4 to 6 hours or overnight. **Bake** 30 to 40 minutes or until custard is set. **Serve** by cutting between sandwiches and lifting sandwiches out of baking dish with wide spatula. **Makes:** 6 sandwiches.

HEARTY WELSH RABBIT

2½ cups milk
¼ cup butter, cubed
¼ cup flour
½ teaspoon salt
¼ teaspoon onion salt

1 teaspoon dry mustard
1½ teaspoons Worcestershire sauce
Dash pepper
8 ounces Cheddar cheese, cubed
Toast or Holland Rusk

Place all ingredients except Cheddar chéese and toast in blender container. **Cover and Process** until blended. With blender continuing to run, **Remove** feeder cap. **Slowly Add** cubed cheese. **Cover and Process** until smooth. **Pour** mixture into saucepan. **Cook** over moderate heat, stirring constantly until thick. **Serve** hot over toast or Holland Rusk. **Makes:** 6 servings.

TOMATO TUNA MOLD

1 package (3 ounces) seasoned
   tomato-flavored gelatin
½ cup hot water
1 can (8 ounces) tomato sauce
1 tablespoon lemon juice
1 cup mayonnaise
1 package (8 ounces) softened
   cream cheese, cubed

2 medium stalks celery,
   cut in 2-inch pieces
½ medium onion, quartered
½ medium green pepper,
   cut in 2-inch pieces
1 can (9¼ ounces) tuna,
   drained and flaked

Place gelatin and hot water in blender container. **Cover and Process** at proper speed for gelatin (low) until gelatin dissolves. **Stop Blender. Add** tomato sauce, lemon juice, mayonnaise and cream cheese. **Cover and Process** until smooth. With blender continuing to run, **Remove** feeder cap and slowly add celery, onion and green pepper. **Cover and Process** until vegetables are coarsely chopped. **Turn** into 5½-cup mold. **Chill** until partially set. **Fold** in tuna. **Chill** until firm. **Makes:** 4 to 6 servings.

SHRIMP TEMPURA

½ cup sifted flour
¼ teaspoon salt
¼ teaspoon baking powder
1 egg
⅓ cup milk

1 tablespoon salad oil
1 pound cooked shrimp, canned or
  frozen
Oil for frying

Place all ingredients except shrimp and oil for frying in blender container. **Cover and Process** until smooth. **Pour** into a bowl. **Heat** one inch of oil in a large skillet to 375°F. **Dip** shrimp in blended batter. **Fry** about 2 or 3 minutes to a golden brown. **Remove** from pan. **Drain** on absorbent paper. **Set Aside** in warm place. **Serve** with Sweet-Sour Sauce*. **Makes:** 3 to 4 servings.

Sweet-Sour Sauce

1½ teaspoons cornstarch
1½ teaspoons sugar
1½ teaspoons soy sauce

2½ tablespoons vinegar
2½ teaspoons pineapple juice

Place all ingredients in blender container. **Cover and Process** until well mixed. **Pour** into saucepan. **Cook** over low heat, stirring constantly about 2 or 3 minutes. **Serve** with shrimp.

CREAMY TUNA SALAD

1 envelope unflavored gelatine
1/4 cup cold water
1 1/4 cups boiling water
2 vegetable bouillon cubes
1 teaspoon lemon juice
1/3 cup mayonnaise
1/4 small onion

1 stalk celery, cut into about
   1-inch pieces
3 sprigs parsley
3 medium stuffed olives
1 can (6 1/2 or 7 ounces) tuna,
   drained

Sprinkle gelatine over cold water in blender container. Allow to stand while assembling remaining ingredients. **Add** boiling water. **Cover and Process** at proper speed for gelatine (low) until gelatine dissolves. If gelatine granules cling to container, use a rubber spatula to push them into the mixture. When gelatine is dissolved, **Add** bouillon cubes with remaining ingredients. **Cover and Process** until ingredients are coarsely chopped. **Turn** into 1-quart mold. **Chill** until firm. **Makes:** 4 servings.

SAUCES

WHITE WINE SAUCE VERONIQUE

½ cup fish broth
3 tablespoons flour
¾ teaspoon salt
¼ teaspoon nutmeg
¼ teaspoon white pepper

4 tablespoons butter, soft
1 cup milk
½ cup dry white Bordeaux wine
2 egg yolks

Place all ingredients except wine and egg yolks in blender container. **Cover and Process** until well blended. **Empty** into saucepan. **Simmer** over low heat, stirring constantly until thickened. Just before serving, **Stir** in wine and egg yolk **(Do Not Boil)**. **Correct** seasoning to taste. **Serve** with fish. **Makes:** 2 cups.

CREAMY SHRIMP SAUCE

1 cup mayonnaise
½ cup sour cream
1 teaspoon dry mustard
1 teaspoon paprika
1 teaspoon lemon juice

½ clove garlic
2 sweet pickles, quartered
2 green onions and tops, cut in 2-inch pieces
1 sprig parsley

Place all ingredients in blender container. **Cover and Process** to mix until smooth. **Refrigerate** until serving. **Serve** with shrimp. **Makes:** 1½ cups.

61

NIPPY CRANBERRY SAUCE

1 can (1 pound) jellied cranberry
   sauce
2 tablespoons honey
1 tablespoon horseradish

1 tablespoon salad oil
1 teaspoon prepared mustard
2 teaspoons Worcestershire sauce

Place all ingredients in blender container. **Cover and Process** until combined. **Refrigerate** until serving. **Makes:** 2 cups.

TARTARE SAUCE

1 cup mayonnaise
1 small dill pickle, quartered
Dash Tabasco

1 slice onion
2 sprigs parsley

Place all ingredients in blender container. **Cover and Process** until pickle, onion, and parsley are finely chopped and ingredients are combined. **Refrigerate** until serving. **Makes:** 1 cup.

INDIAN CURRY SAUCE

1 cup mayonnaise
½ cup catsup
2 anchovies
⅛ green pepper, cut in pieces

2 green onions, cut in 1-inch pieces
4 parsley leaves
1 tablespoon curry powder
⅛ teaspoon cayenne pepper

Place all ingredients in blender container. **Cover and Process** at high speed until smooth. **Chill and Serve** with lamb, fowl, or fish. **Makes** 1½ cups.

DILL SAUCE

1 medium-sized dill pickle, cut in
   1-inch pieces
Salt and pepper to taste

½ cup sour cream
1 tablespoon prepared mustard

Place all ingredients in blender container. **Cover and Process** until smooth. **Serve** with hamburger, ham or pork roast. **Makes:** ½ cup.

DRESSINGS

GREEN MAYONNAISE

12 spinach leaves
12 watercress leaves
 8 sprigs parsley
 9 sprigs fresh chervil

9 sprigs fresh tarragon
1 clove garlic, halved
1 cup mayonnaise

Blanch fresh greens in boiling water 2 minutes. **Drain,** reserving 2 tablespoons liquid. **Rub** inside of blender container with cut side of garlic and discard. **Place** blanched greens and liquid in blender container and process 30 seconds to purée. **Stir** into mayonnaise. **Chill. Serve** on chilled fish or vegetable salad. **Makes:** 1⅓ cups. Note: 1 teaspoon dried chervil leaves and dried tarragon leaves may be substituted for fresh herbs. Stir into mayonnaise with blanched greens.

BLENDER BLUE CHEESE DRESSING

½ cup evaporated milk
½ cup salad oil
 1 teaspoon onion salt

2 ounces (⅓ cup) blue cheese
3 tablespoons cider vinegar

Place all ingredients in blender container. **Cover and Process** a few seconds until smooth and thickened. **Chill,** tightly covered, in refrigerator. **Serve** over wedges of lettuce, crisp mixed greens, sliced tomatoes, tomato aspic, or as a dressing on open-face sandwiches of sliced chicken, turkey or ham. **Makes:** about 1½ cups.

PIQUANT HERB FRENCH DRESSING

¾ cup corn oil
¼ cup cider vinegar
 1 tablespoon tarragon vinegar
White of 1 hard-cooked egg
 2 teaspoons capers

½ teaspoon salt
½ teaspoon prepared mustard
Dash pepper
 2 small sprigs parsley
 1 blade chive

Place all ingredients in blender container in order given. **Cover and Process** 30 to 40 seconds until mixture is slightly thickened. **Makes:** about 1 cup.

ONION DELICATE

1 can (10½ ounces) condensed
   cream of vegetable soup
¼ to ⅓ cup milk
Dash black pepper

3 small white onions, cooked
4 tablespoons butter
1 teaspoon chopped chives or
1 tablespoon Parmesan cheese
   for garnish

Place soup, milk, pepper and onions in blender container. **Cover and Process** until smooth. **Pour** into saucepan. **Add** butter. **Cook** slowly, over low heat, until butter is melted and sauce is hot. **Add** 1 teaspoon chopped chives or 1 tablespoon grated Parmesan, if desired. **Serve** over cooked broccoli, asparagus, potatoes or cauliflower or as a sauce for cooked fish steaks or fillets. **Makes:** about 1½ cups.

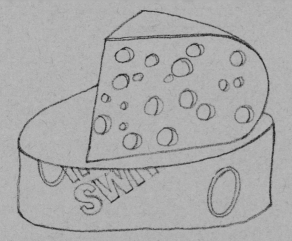

ROQUEFORT DRESSING

1 pint sour cream
½ cup mayonnaise
2 tablespoons wine vinegar
1 slice onion

1 small clove garlic, split
1 teaspoon salt
8 ounces Roquefort cheese

Place all ingredients except cheese in blender container. **Cover and Process** until smooth. With blender continuing to run, **Remove** feeder cap and slowly add Roquefort. **Cover and Process** until combined. **Refrigerate** until serving. **Makes:** 3½ cups.

AVOCADO DRESSING

1 ripe avocado, peeled and diced
Juice of 1 lemon
Peel of 1 lemon

2 tablespoons honey
¼ teaspoon salt
½ cup heavy cream

Place all ingredients except cream in blender container. **Cover and Process** until smooth. With blender continuing to run, **Remove** feeder cap and slowly add cream. **Stop Blender** and scrape down sides of container with rubber spatula, if necessary. **Cover and Process** until smooth and fluffy. **Refrigerate** until serving. **Makes:** 1 cup.

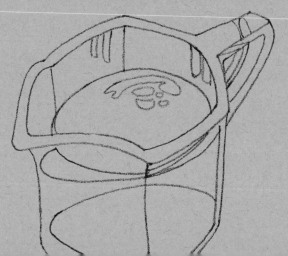

BREADS

FRUIT AND NUT BREAD

1¼ cups sifted flour
1 teaspoon baking powder
½ teaspoon salt
½ teaspoon soda
1 cup whole bran
½ cup walnuts
2 eggs

⅓ cup shortening
⅔ cup sugar
¼ cup buttermilk
3 ripe bananas, sliced in ½-inch pieces
1 cup dried apricots

Preheat oven to 350°F. Grease 9x5x3-inch loaf pan. **Sift** together flour, baking powder, salt and soda in medium bowl. **Add** whole bran. **Place** nuts in blender container. **Cover and Process** until coarsely chopped. **Add** to flour mixture. **Place** eggs, shortening, sugar and milk in blender container. **Cover and Process** until well blended. With blender continuing to run, **Remove** feeder cap and slowly add bananas. **Cover and Process** until completely liquefied. **Add** apricots. **Cover and Process** until apricots are coarsely chopped. **Add** to dry ingredients. **Stir** well. **Turn** into prepared pan. **Bake** 45 minutes or until cake tester inserted comes out clean. **Makes:** 1 loaf.

APPLE PANCAKES

1 egg
1 tablespoon sugar
1 tablespoon softened butter

1 medium apple, peeled, cored and
   quartered
1 cup evaporated milk
1 cup packaged pancake mix

Place egg, sugar, butter, apple and evaporated milk in blender container. **Cover and Process** a few seconds until apple is chopped. **Add** pancake mix. **Cover and Process** a few seconds longer until blended. **Pour** about ¼ cup at a time onto preheated hot (400°F) electric griddle. **Bake** until bubbles appear on top and underside is browned. **Turn** and bake to brown second side. **Serve** hot with Cinnamon Cream Syrup.* **Makes:** 4 to 5 servings.

Cinnamon Cream Syrup

1 cup light corn syrup
2 cups sugar
½ cup water

2 teaspoons cinnamon
1 cup evaporated milk

Combine corn syrup, sugar, water and cinnamon in medium size saucepan. **Bring** to a full boil over medium heat, stirring constantly. **Continue Stirring** and boiling for an additional 2 minutes. **Cook** 5 minutes. **Stir** in evaporated milk. **Serve** warm over Apple Pancakes. **Makes:** about 3 cups.

POPOVERS

1 cup milk

2 eggs

1 cup sifted flour

½ teaspoon salt

Preheat oven to 450°F. **Place** all ingredients in blender container. **Cover and Process** until smooth. **Fill** greased muffin tins or custard cups ½ full. **Bake** 10 minutes. **Lower** oven heat to 350°F. and bake 35 minutes. **Serve** while hot. **Makes:** 8 popovers.

CRANBERRY-NUT BREAD

2 cups sifted flour
1½ teaspoons baking powder
½ teaspoon soda
1 egg
¼ cup shortening
1 teaspoon salt

1 1x2-inch piece orange rind
1 cup sugar
¾ cup orange juice
½ cup nuts
1 cup cranberries

Preheat oven to 350°F. Grease loaf pan. **Sift** flour, baking powder and baking soda into mixing bowl. **Place** egg, shortening, salt, orange rind, sugar and orange juice in blender container. **Cover and Process** until rind is grated fine. **Add** nuts and cranberries. **Cover and Process** until chopped. **Empty** into flour mixture and mix only until blended. **Spoon** into prepared pan. **Bake** 50-60 minutes or until cake tester inserted comes out clean. **Makes:** 1 loaf.

CHEESE MUFFINS

2 cups sifted flour
4 teaspoons baking powder
1 tablespoon sugar
½ teaspoon salt

1 egg
1 cup milk
3 tablespoons soft butter
½ pound sharp Cheddar cheese, cubed

Preheat oven to 350°F. Grease muffin tins well. **Sift** flour, baking powder, sugar and salt into mixing bowl. **Place** egg, milk, and butter in blender container. **Cover and Process** until well blended. With blender continuing to run, **Remove** feeder cap and slowly add cheese. **Cover and Process** until cheese is finely chopped. **Pour** into dry ingredients and mix only until flour is moistened. **Fill** prepared tins ⅔ full. **Bake** 15 to 25 minutes or until muffins test done. **Makes:** 12 muffins.

FRUIT COCKTAIL FRITTERS

1½ cups sifted flour
1½ teaspoons baking powder
½ teaspoon salt
1 tablespoon sugar

½ cup milk
2 eggs
1 cup well-drained fruit cocktail
Fat for frying

Heat fat to 375°F. **Sift** dry ingredients together. **Place** milk and eggs in blender container. **Cover and Process** until well mixed. **Stop Blender. Add** flour mixture. **Cover and Process** until dry ingredients are just moistened. **Stir** in well-drained fruit. **Drop** batter from tablespoon into hot fat. **Fry** until golden brown on all sides. **Drain. Serve** while hot as a hot bread, with butter or syrup. **Makes:** about 15 fritters.

BLUEBERRY PANCAKES

1 cup sifted flour	1 egg
½ teaspoon baking soda	1 cup buttermilk
¾ teaspoon baking powder	1 tablespoon butter, melted
½ cup fresh, canned or frozen blueberries, drained	½ teaspoon salt

Sift flour, soda and baking powder into a mixing bowl. **Add** blueberries. **Place** remaining ingredients in blender container. **Cover and Process** until thoroughly blended. **Add** to dry ingredients. **Mix** just enough to dampen the dry ingredients (leave lumpy). **Drop** by tablespoonfuls onto a lightly greased griddle. **Bake** until brown. **Turn** only once. **Makes:** 8 to 10 pancakes.

CAKES, PIES & COOKIES

CREAM CHEESE PIE

16 graham crackers
½ cup sugar
¼ cup melted butter
 2 eggs
Rind of 1 lemon

⅛ teaspoon salt
¾ cup sugar
 4 3-ounce packages cream cheese,
   softened to room temperature

Preheat oven to 350°F. **Break** half of crackers into blender container. **Cover and Process** to crumb. **Empty** into bowl. **Repeat** with remaining crackers. **Add** ½ cup sugar and butter to crumbs. **Mix** lightly until moistened. **Press** into 9-inch pie pan. **Place** eggs, lemon rind, salt and ¾ cup sugar in blender container. **Break** softened cream cheese in pieces and add to mixture in blender container. **Cover and Process** on high speed until smooth. **Stop Blender** and scrape down sides of container with rubber spatula, if necessary. **Turn** mixture into pie shell. **Bake** 40 to 60 minutes or until firm. **Makes:** 8 servings.

BERRY TORTE

16 graham crackers
½ cup sugar
¼ cup melted butter
2 eggs
1 package (8 ounces) cream cheese, softened, cut in fourths

1 cup sugar
1 package frozen berries (strawberries, raspberries, blueberries)
1 tablespoon lemon juice
½ cup sugar
1 tablespoon cornstarch

Preheat oven to 350°F. **Break** half of graham crackers in blender container. **Cover and Process** to crumb. **Empty** into a bowl. **Repeat** with remaining crackers. **Add** ½ cup sugar and butter to crumbs in bowl. **Mix** lightly until moistened. **Press** into a 9x9x2-inch pan. **Place** eggs and softened cream cheese in blender container. **Cover and Process** until smooth. **Stop Blender** and scrape down sides of container with rubber spatula, if necessary. With blender continuing to run, **Remove** feeder cap and slowly add 1 cup sugar. **Cover and Process** until well blended. **Spread** cream cheese mixture over crust. **Bake** 25 to 30 minutes or until firm. **Cool. Meanwhile Drain** juice from berries.

Mix berry liquid with lemon juice, ½ cup sugar and cornstarch in small saucepan. **Cook** over medium heat until mixture is thick and clear. **Add** berries. **Spread** over cheese mixture. **Chill** before serving. **Makes:** 6 to 8 servings.

CHOCOLATE CHIFFON PIE

1 package (6 ounces) semi-sweet chocolate pieces
⅓ cup sugar
⅓ cup very hot water

1 teaspoon vanilla
4 eggs, separated
1 9-inch baked pie crust

Place chocolate, sugar, water and vanilla in blender container. **Cover and Process** until smooth. With blender continuing to run, **Remove** feeder cap and slowly add egg yolks. **Increase** to high speed and process about 60 seconds until thick. **Beat** egg whites until stiff peaks form. **Carefully fold** chocolate mixture into egg whites with wire whisk or rubber spatula. **Fold** only until combined. **Turn** into baked pie shell. **Refrigerate** until firm. **Makes:** 8 servings.

BITTERSWEET BROWNIES

1½ cups pecans
½ cup flour
1 teaspoon baking powder
½ teaspoon salt
2 eggs

½ cup soft butter
1 cup sugar
1 teaspoon vanilla extract
2 squares unsweetened chocolate, melted

Preheat oven to 350°F. Grease a 9-inch pan. **Place** pecans in blender container. **Cover and Process** as for nuts. **Empty** on waxed paper. **Sift** flour, baking powder and salt on waxed paper and set aside. **Place** eggs, butter, sugar and vanilla in blender container. **Cover and Process** at high speed until smooth. **Remove** feeder cap and add melted chocolate. **Cover and Process** until smooth. **Add** flour mixture gradually through feeder cap. **Stop Blender** and add nuts. **Mix** into batter with rubber spatula. **Spread** in prepared pan. **Bake** 20 to 30 minutes or until cake tests done. **Cool and Frost** with Bittersweet Chocolate Frosting.*

*Bittersweet Chocolate Frosting

2 squares unsweetened chocolate, cut in small pieces

2 tablespoons butter

4 tablespoons hot milk

1 cup powdered sugar

1 teaspoon vanilla

Place all ingredients in blender container. **Cover and Process** until completely smooth. If frosting is too thick add a small amount of cream. **Spread** over brownies. **Cool.** Cut in 1½-inch squares.

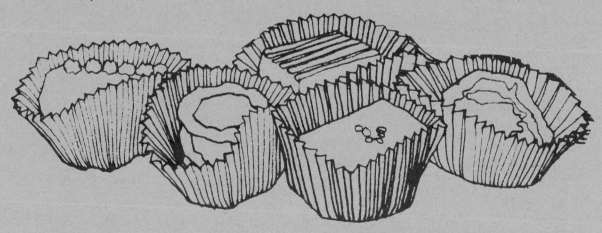

COCOA-APPLESAUCE CAKE

2 cups sifted cake flour
2 tablespoons cocoa
1 teaspoon salt
1½ teaspoons baking powder
½ teaspoon soda
1 teaspoon cinnamon
½ teaspoon cloves

½ teaspoon nutmeg
½ teaspoon allspice
2 eggs
½ cup shortening
1¾ cups sugar
¾ cup raisins
3 medium apples, cored and cubed

Preheat oven to 350°F. Grease and wax paper line 13x9x2-inch pan. **Sift** flour, cocoa, salt, baking powder, soda and spices in medium mixing bowl. **Place** eggs, shortening, sugar and raisins in blender container. **Cover and Process** at high speed until smooth. **Stop Blender** and scrape down sides of container with rubber spatula, if necessary. With blender continuing to run, **Remove** feeder cap and slowly add apples. **Cover and Process** until smooth. **Pour** mixture over dry ingredients. **Mix** well. **Turn** batter into prepared pan. **Bake** 45 minutes or until cake tester inserted comes out clean. **Makes:** 1 cake.

ALMOND CRISPIES

½ cup whole almonds
½ cup butter or margarine
1 cup brown sugar, packed
2 eggs
½ cup sifted all-purpose flour

1 teaspoon baking powder
¼ teaspoon salt
1 teaspoon cinnamon
¾ cup fine dry bread crumbs
¼ cup fresh dates, finely cut

Preheat oven to 350°F. **Process** almonds in blender container to grind. **Cream** butter and sugar thoroughly in mixing bowl. **Add** eggs. **Beat** well. **Sift** flour with baking powder, salt and cinnamon. **Add** to creamed mixture and blend well. **Stir** in almonds, crumbs and dates. **Drop** by small spoonfuls onto ungreased cooky sheet about 3 inches apart. **Bake** 12 to 15 minutes. **Makes:** about 4 dozen.

CHRISTMAS BRUNCH CAKE

1 cup pecans
¼ cup melted butter
¼ cup white sugar
⅓ cup brown sugar
1 teaspoon cinnamon
14 green maraschino cherries,
    well drained
2¼ cups sifted flour

1 teaspoon baking powder
1 teaspoon baking soda
½ teaspoon salt
2 eggs
½ cup soft shortening
1 cup sugar
1 teaspoon vanilla extract
1 cup sour cream

Preheat oven to 350°F. Grease a "Turban" or "Baba" mold or similar fluted tube mold very well. **Place** pecans in blender container. **Cover and Process** to chop. **Empty** into small bowl and combine with butter, sugars and cinnamon. **Press** mixture on bottom and sides of prepared mold. **Place** cherries into blender container. **Cover and Process** as for nuts. Spread on absorbent paper to remove as much moisture as possible. **Sift** flour, baking powder, baking soda and salt together in large mixing bowl. **Add** cherries and mix well to distribute cherries throughout. **Place** eggs, shortening, sugar and vanilla in blender container. **Cover and Process** at high speed until mixture is smooth. **Add** sour cream and continue to process only until thoroughly blended. **Pour** over flour mixture. **Stir** well to combine all ingredients. **Spoon** into mold, spreading evenly. **Bake** 45 to 55 minutes or until cake tests done. **Cool** 5 minutes before removing from pan. **Makes:** 1 cake.

DESSERTS

RASPBERRY MACAROON MOUSSE

2 packages frozen raspberries, thawed
2 cups heavy cream
2 egg whites

½ cup sugar
⅔ cup crisp macaroon crumbs

Place raspberries in blender container. **Cover and Process** until puréed. **Strain and Pour** into mixing bowl. **Place** cream into chilled blender container. **Cover and Beat** at low speed. **Remove** and fold into raspberries. **Beat** egg whites with rotary beater, gradually adding sugar. **Continue Beating** until stiff but not dry. **Fold** into cream mixture. **Spoon** into 2-quart mold. **Place** in freezer 1 hour. **Place** few macaroon cookies in blender container. **Cover and Process** until ⅔ cup crumbs are produced. **Cover** mousse with crumbs. **Swirl** with knife to form streaks. **Continue** freezing until firm. **Makes:** 6 servings.

PINEAPPLE CHEESE SOUFFLE

¼ cup dairy sour cream
2 cups pineapple creamed
   cottage cheese
⅓ cup flour
Dash salt

6 tablespoons sugar, divided
1½ teaspoons lemon juice
3 egg yolks, well beaten
4 egg whites
Pineapple Sauce*

Preheat oven to 300°F. **Place** sour cream in blender container. **Add** cottage cheese, a half cup at a time. **Process** until smooth. **Add** flour and process until smooth. **Beat** salt, 4 tablespoons sugar and lemon juice into egg yolks in mixing bowl. **Combine** sour cream-cheese mixture and yolk mixture well. **Beat** egg whites until soft peaks form. **Add** 2 tablespoons sugar, one tablespoon at a time. **Continue to Beat** until whites are stiff but not dry. **Fold** whites into rest of mixture. **Turn** into 6-cup, 3¼-inch deep baking

dish. **Bake** 1 hour 20 minutes or until firm. **Serve** at once with chilled Pineapple Sauce.*
Makes: 6 servings.

Pineapple Sauce

2 teaspoons cornstarch
6 tablespoons canned pineapple syrup
6 tablespoons cold water
¼ cup light corn syrup

¼ teaspoon lemon juice
Yellow food coloring
⅔ cup chilled, canned, well-drained
    pineapple tidbits

Combine cornstarch, pineapple syrup, water, corn syrup and lemon juice in saucepan.
Cook over medium heat, stirring constantly until sauce thickens slightly. **Remove** from
heat. **Stir** in few drops of food coloring. **Refrigerate. Add** pineapple tidbits just before
serving. **Pour** over pineapple cheese souffle. **Makes:** 1½ cups.

BROADWAY BAVARIANS

Vanilla layer:

1 envelope unflavored gelatine
¼ cup cold milk
½ cup milk, heated to boiling
1 egg
¼ cup sugar

⅛ teaspoon salt
1 teaspoon vanilla
½ cup heavy cream
¾ cup ice cubes or crushed ice

Sprinkle gelatine over cold milk in blender container. **Cover and Process** at proper speed for gelatine (low) until gelatine is softened. **Remove** feeder cap from blender container and add boiling milk. **Continue to Process** until gelatine dissolves. If gelatine granules cling to container, use a rubber spatula to push them into the mixture. When gelatine is dissolved, **Add** egg, sugar, salt and vanilla. **Cover and Process** to whip. **Add** cream, then ice cubes one at a time. **Process** as for ice cubes until melted. **Pour** immediately into six 8-ounce glasses or eight 6-ounce glasses. Rinse blender container and prepare chocolate layer.

Chocolate layer:

1 envelope unflavored gelatine
¼ cup cold milk
½ cup milk, heated to boiling
1 egg
2 tablespoons sugar

⅛ teaspoon salt
½ cup semi-sweet chocolate pieces
½ teaspoon vanilla
½ cup heavy cream
¾ cup ice cubes or crushed ice

Sprinkle gelatine over cold milk into blender container. **Cover and Process** at proper speed for gelatine (low) until gelatine is softened. **Remove** feeder cap from blender container and add boiling milk. **Cover and Process** until gelatine dissolves. If gelatine granules cling to container, use a rubber spatula to push them into the mixture. When gelatine is dissolved, **Add** egg, sugar and salt. **Add** chocolate pieces and process at highest speed until smooth. **Add** vanilla, cream and ice cubes one at a time. **Process** as for ice cubes until melted. **Pour** at once over vanilla layer in glasses. Allow to set 15 minutes before serving. **Garnish** with additional whipped cream, if desired. **Makes:** 5 to 8 servings.

MINT CREAM

2 envelopes unflavored gelatine	⅛ teaspoon salt
2½ cups milk, divided	¼ cup green creme de menthe
2 eggs	1 cup heavy cream
⅔ cup sugar	Sprigs of mint for garnish

Sprinkle gelatine over ½ cup milk in blender container. Allow to soften while assembling remaining ingredients. **Bring** one cup milk to full boil. **Pour** into blender container. **Cover and Process** at low speed for 10 seconds and high for 20 seconds. **Add** remaining 1 cup milk, eggs, sugar, salt and green creme de menthe. **Cover and Process** at high speed for 15 seconds. **Turn** into mixing bowl and stir in cream. **Turn** into 5-cup mold, bowl or individual serving dishes. **Chill** until firm, about 3 hours. **Garnish** with sprigs of mint, if desired. **Makes:** 8 servings.

CARAMEL FLAN

1¾ cups sugar, divided
8 eggs

3⅓ cups evaporated milk
2 teaspoons vanilla

Preheat oven to 350°F. **Place** 1 cup sugar into an 8-inch square pan in which the custard is to be baked. **Cook,** stirring constantly, over medium heat until sugar melts and is light amber. **Tip** the pan around until it is entirely coated with the caramel mixture. **Cool. Place** eggs, milk, remaining sugar and vanilla into blender container. **Cover and Process** until well mixed. **Turn** into caramel-coated pan. **Cover** and place in a larger pan. **Pour** in 1 inch of hot water. **Bake** 1 hour or until knife inserted near edge of custard comes out clean. **Unmold** immediately. **Makes:** 9 servings.

CHOCOLATE CREAM

2 envelopes unflavored gelatine	⅛ teaspoon salt
½ cup cold milk	1 teaspoon vanilla
¾ cup sugar	1 cup heavy cream
⅓ cup cocoa	1½ cups crushed ice
1 cup milk	Whipped cream, almonds,
1 egg	chocolate curls

Sprinkle gelatine over cold milk in blender container. **Cover and Process** at proper speed for gelatine (low) until gelatine is softened. **Mix** sugar and cocoa in saucepan. **Stir** in milk. **Bring** to a boil, stirring constantly. **Remove** feeder cap from blender container and add hot cocoa mixture. **Process** at highest speed until gelatine dissolves. **Add** egg, salt, vanilla, cream and ice. **Process** to liquefy. **Turn** at once into serving bowl. Allow to set 5 minutes before serving. **Garnish** with additional whipped cream, toasted slivered almonds and chocolate curls. **Makes:** 8 servings.

CHOCOLATE RUM PARFAITS

2 envelopes unflavored gelatine
¼ cup cold milk
6 tablespoons dark rum
¾ cup milk, heated to boiling
1 egg
¼ cup sugar
⅛ teaspoon salt

1 package (6 ounces) semi-sweet chocolate pieces
2 cups heavy cream, divided
1½ cups ice cubes or crushed ice
1 teaspoon vanilla
½ cup chopped toasted pecans

Sprinkle gelatine over milk and rum in blender container. Allow to stand while assembling other ingredients. **Add** boiling milk. **Cover and Process** at proper speed for gelatine (low) until gelatine dissolves. If gelatine granules cling to container, use a rubber spatula to push them into the mixture. **Add** egg, sugar and salt. **Turn** control to high speed. **Add** chocolate and process until smooth. **Add** 1 cup cream. **Add** ice cubes one at a time and process as for ice cubes until melted. **Let Stand** 15 minutes to thicken. **Add** vanilla to remaining 1 cup cream and whip until stiff. **Alternate** chocolate mixture, whipped cream and chopped pecans in parfait glasses. Serve immediately or chill. **Makes:** 8 servings.

PEACH MELBA MOLD

2 envelopes unflavored gelatine
½ cup cold milk
1 cup milk, heated to boiling
½ lemon, peeled and seeded
½ cup sugar

⅛ teaspoon salt
1 package (12 ounces) frozen
  peaches, thawed
1 cup heavy cream
1 cup ice cubes or crushed ice

Sprinkle gelatine over cold milk in blender container that will hold 5 cups. Allow to stand while assembling remaining ingredients. **Add** boiling milk. **Cover and Process** at proper speed for gelatine (low) until gelatine dissolves. **Add** lemon, sugar, salt, peaches and cream. **Cover and Process** at high speed until smooth. **Add** ice cubes one at a time. **Process** as for ice cubes until melted. **Turn** into 5-cup mold, bowl or individual serving dishes. **Chill** until firm, about 2-3 hours. **Unmold** and serve with Melba Sauce.* **Makes:** 6 servings.

Note: If blender container will not hold 5 cups, do not add cream to blender. After ice cubes are melted, quickly pour gelatine mixture into a bowl and beat in cream.

Melba Sauce

1 package (10 ounces) frozen
  raspberries, thawed

Place raspberries in blender container. **Cover and Process** to a purée. **Strain. Makes:**
¾ cup.

PEACH ICE CREAM

4 to 6 ripe peaches (or ½ cup   1 cup heavy cream
  peach puree)   1 cup confectioners sugar
1 tablespoon lemon juice

Peel peaches and remove pits. **Place** peaches and lemon juice in blender container
Cover and Process to purée. **Stop Blender** and scrape down sides of container with rubber spatula, if necessary **Whip** cream until it holds a soft peak. **Add** powdered sugar
and continue to beat until stiff. **Fold** in peach purée. **Turn** into refrigerator trays.
Freeze approximately 2 to 4 hours until firm. **Makes:** 2 trays ice cream.

CHOCOLATE MINI-MOUSSE

¼ cup cold water
2 envelopes unflavored gelatine
¾ cup boiling water
⅓ cup instant nonfat dry milk
  (dry form)

¼ cup sugar
1 package (6 ounces) semi-sweet
  chocolate pieces
2 cups crushed ice

Sprinkle gelatine over cold water in blender container. **Process** at proper speed for gelatine (low) until gelatine is softened. **Add** boiling water. **Cover and Process** until gelatine dissolves. **Add** nonfat dry milk, sugar and chocolate pieces. **Process** at high speed until chips are melted. **Add** crushed ice and process until mixture begins to thicken, about 1 minute. **Pour** immediately into dessert dishes. **Makes:** 4 servings.

CINNAMON-APPLE ICE CREAM

1 envelope unflavored gelatine
½ cup boiling water
1 can (6 ounces) frozen apple juice
   (concentrated)
6 ounces cold water

2 tart eating apples, peeled, cored,
   cut in quarters
1 teaspoon lemon juice
1 teaspoon cinnamon
½ to ¾ cup sugar
1 cup heavy cream

Sprinkle gelatine into boiling water. **Stir** until dissolved. **Place** gelatine and remaining ingredients, except heavy cream, in blender container. **Cover and Process** until apples are chopped. **Stop Blender** and scrape down sides of container with rubber spatula, if necessary. **Whip** cream until stiff. **Fold** in gelatine mixture. **Pour** into 2 freezer trays. **Freeze** about 4 hours until firm. **Makes:** 2 trays ice cream.

DESSERT SAUCES

QUICK BUTTERSCOTCH SAUCE

½ cup light cream
1½ cups granulated brown sugar
2 tablespoons soft butter

1 teaspoon vanilla extract
⅛ teaspoon salt

Place all ingredients in blender container. **Cover and Process** at high speed until smooth. **Store** in covered jar in refrigerator. **Serve** over ice cream. **Makes:** 2 cups.

BLENDER BERRY SAUCE

1 package (10 ounces) frozen
  raspberries or strawberries, thawed

½ cup orange juice
1 tablespoon cornstarch

Combine all ingredients in blender container. **Cover and Process** at high speed until ingredients are well blended, about 1 minute. **Pour** into saucepan. Bring to full boil, stirring constantly. **Boil** 1 minute. **Serve** warm over ice cream or cake. **Makes:** 1¼ cups.

CARAMEL SAUCE

¾ cup brown sugar
2 tablespoons soft butter

¼ teaspoon salt
½ cup hot evaporated milk

Place all ingredients in blender container. **Cover and Process** on low speed until sugar is dissolved. **Makes:** 1¼ cups.

CHOCOLATE SAUCE

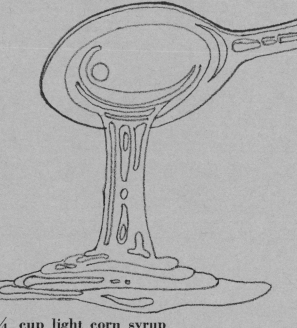

2 squares unsweetened chocolate,
  cut into pieces
¼ cup sugar
  Dash of salt

¼ cup light corn syrup
⅓ cup hot milk
½ teaspoon vanilla extract

Place all ingredients in blender container. **Cover and Process** until chocolate is liquefied and sauce is thick and creamy. **Makes:** ¾ cup.

DRINKS

NECTARINE DAIQUIRI

1 fresh nectarine, peeled, pitted and diced

2 teaspoons sugar

2 tablespoons lime juice

½ cup light rum

1 to 1½ cups finely crushed ice

Place nectarine, sugar, lime juice and rum in blender container. **Cover and Process** until smooth. **Add** ice and process until frappéed. **Serve** in chilled champagne glasses. **Makes:** 3 to 4 daiquiris.

QUEEN OF THE ISLANDS

¾ cup orange juice

¼ cup lime juice

2 tablespoons sugar

1 egg white, unbeaten

1 cup sweet white wine

1 cup crushed ice or 4 whole ice cubes

Combine juices and sugar in blender container. **Cover and Process** on low speed until sugar is liquefied. **Stop Blender. Add** egg white, wine and ice. **Cover and Process** on high speed only until ice is liquefied. **Pour** into cocktail glasses. **Makes:** eight 3-ounce cocktails.

CZARINA'S DELIGHT

2 tablespoons lemon juice
1 cup grape juice
2 tablespoons sugar

2 jiggers vodka
1 egg white, unbeaten
1 cup crushed ice or 4 whole ice cubes

Place juices and sugar in blender container. **Cover and Process** on low until sugar is liquefied. **Stop Blender. Add** egg white, vodka and ice. **Cover and Process** on high speed only until ice is liquefied. **Pour** into cocktail glasses. **Makes:** six 3-ounce cocktails.

ROSE COOL BLOSSOM

1 can (6 ounces) frozen lemonade
   concentrate, undiluted

1½ cups rose wine
1 cup crushed ice or
   4 whole ice cubes

Place all ingredients in blender container. **Cover and Process** at high speed until ice is liquefied. **Pour** into cocktail glasses. **Makes:** eight 3-ounce drinks.

GRASSHOPPER

2 jiggers white creme de cacao
1 jigger creme de menthe

1 jigger heavy cream
¾ cup crushed ice or 3 whole ice cubes

Place all ingredients in blender container. **Cover and Process** at high speed until smooth. **Strain** into cocktail glasses. **Makes:** two 3-ounce drinks.

CRICKET

2 jiggers brown creme de cacao
1 jigger brandy

½ pint vanilla ice cream, softened
1 cup crushed ice or 4 whole ice cubes

Place all ingredients in blender container. **Cover and Process** at high speed until ice is frappéed. **Serve** in cocktail glasses. **Makes:** 2 tall drinks.

BACARDI

⅓ cup frozen limeade concentrate, thawed
4 jiggers light rum

1½ cups crushed ice or
6 whole ice cubes
3 tablespoons grenadine

Place all ingredients in blender container. **Cover and Process** at high speed a few seconds. **Strain** into cocktail glasses. **Makes:** four 3-ounce drinks.

DAIQUIRI

⅓ cup frozen limeade concentrate
4 jiggers light rum

1½ cups crushed ice or
6 whole ice cubes

Place all ingredients in blender container. **Cover and Process** as for ice cubes, a few seconds. **Strain** into cocktail glasses. **Makes:** four 3-ounce drinks.

INDEX